How to be a Totally Awesome Employee

by Melody Litton

Illustrated by Jake Croft

For the totally awesome employees out there;

thank you for your guiding light

We've seen good, bad, better, and best. But if we're lucky, we've also seen totally awesome.

Totally awesome employees do exist. They make the workplace (and the world) a better place to be.

Totally awesome employees make a difference. This book holds the secrets to their awesomeness. As we study them and learn their ways, we will be lifted to greater heights.

Each of us has the potential to become a totally awesome employee. It's a journey worth pursuing and one that can begin today. Those who choose to become a totally awesome employee choose happiness and success; not only in the workplace but also in life.

Melody Litton

Totally Awesome Employees

Melody Litton

AWESOME!

NOT AWESOME!

Totally Awesome Employees

Show Up

"I am the epitome of reliability."

Rule one: Show up. Really, I mean it. Totally awesome employees show up for work.

I was a hiring manager at one point and had interviewed eight people for a particular position. After second interviews for three of the eight, I chose one individual and extended a job offer. He had presented himself extremely well and I was anxious to have him on the team. He left my office after filling out paperwork and shaking my hand.

Monday morning came but he didn't. There was no call, no follow up letter explaining why. Nothing. I watched the paper for a couple days and took note of accidents and the obituaries; figuring I'd give him the benefit of the doubt. But on the fourth day, just for curiosity's sake, I gave him a call from a private line. He picked up and sounded A OK. I didn't bother to talk to him or ask why. I just hung up my phone and chalked another mark on the totally non-awesome employee chart.

He may have had a great excuse for not being there. But there is never a great excuse for not extending a courtesy call and leaving an employer hanging. Unless of course you're dead. Even then, a message written on a steamy bathroom mirror would be appreciated- I've heard ghosts can do such things.

Rhonda owned a small business with only a handful of employees. Everyone had specific jobs to do and schedules which complemented one another beautifully. The workload was fair and the pay more than decent. Rhonda had hired a new employee recently. This woman had come to her seeking work and had literally begged for the job. Knowing how badly the woman needed work, Rhonda offered her employment and placed her on the schedule. Within two weeks, the once clean and efficient schedule looked more like a doodle page of an elementary student. The new hire was switching shifts and leaving early and other times not showing up at all. There were Xs and arrows and lines all over the page. The other employees were disgruntled and the workload was no longer fair.

Was she a cancer patient who needed special accommodations or maybe a mother of four sick children? Perhaps she had been knocked in the head and dealt with short term memory loss? Nope. None of the above or even anything near it. Rather; she "slept in", "preferred seeing the dentist in the morning", "just wasn't up to it that day", or "ripped a nail off and needed to get it fixed", and "really ought to take my friend out for ice cream for his birthday". Other days there was no excuse at all, not even a pathetically lame one.

Jennifer worked at an adult family home caring for five disabled men. She was hired to work four overnight shifts a week. What she ended up working was closer to 28 nights a month as well as days, often 72 hours straight without any breaks.

When her shift ended at 7 AM, no one would show up to take over. When it was her night scheduled to be off, her employer would plead with her to work because the scheduled employee had some other matter they felt was more pressing than actually coming to work. Jennifer loved her clients and wanted them to be taken care of. But trying to make up for every non-awesome employee was literally killing her. One can only go so many nights without sleep and days without a break. Even totally awesome employees are human.

When employees fail to show up, employers and co-workers are negatively affected. It's hard on the company, the clients, and everyone else involved. When a person takes a position with a company, no matter how large or how small, that person agrees to better that company. Failure to show up shows failure of integrity.

Totally awesome employees show up. They can be counted on to be there. When a legitimate need arises to miss work or to be late, an employer is willing to accommodate them due to their great track record. Totally awesome employees care about their company, their co-workers, and the clients they serve. They recognize how their choices and reliability affect everyone else.

Melody Litton

Totally Awesome Employees

Aren't Jerk-faces

"I radiate kindness and light to all around me."

"Stop being a jerk-face!" This is what my children yell when one of them is being particularly rude, ornery, or just really un-fun to be around. And although I don't condone name calling, when someone *is* being a jerk-face I may close my ears when they get called out about it. And I've used the term here and there when warranted.

Totally awesome employees don't roll their eyes, make rude comments, and treat others as though they are annoyances. They don't say mean things, stir up contention, or act as though they are better than everyone else. They aren't hateful, angry, ornery, or bad-tempered. They aren't life-drainers, soul-suckers, darkness-bringers, drama-makers, or conflict-stimulators. In a nut-shell, they aren't jerk-faces.

Amanda is beautiful. She wears a smile, laughs easily, and is fun to be around. She is intelligent and witty, swift to give compliments and quick to meet the needs of others. She listens when spoken to and carries on conversations with ease.

Amanda is a server at a small town cafe and has been for ten years. The food is decent and the decor just ok. But she is outstanding and customers love her. They come back again and again because of how they are treated and how they feel when they are there.

Totally awesome employees radiate light. They smile. They are kind. They do their best to bring happiness to the world and to treat others like they matter. They respect themselves and they represent their employers well.

Some employees have bad attitudes or behave rudely. They talk smack, degrade those around them, act annoyed they have to do their job, slack off, don't care about anything but themselves, or criticize at every opportunity. Then they wonder why they are miserable, why customers don't respond well to them and co-workers don't seem to like them.

Totally awesome employees are the individuals every employer dreams of, every co-worker hopes for, and every customer appreciates. They are the opposite of jerk-faces.

Totally Awesome Employees

Don't Need Babysitters

"I am responsible and mature. I perform to the best of my ability at all times."

Kellie was conducting interviews for a new management position within her company. It was one which required a lot of creativity, self-motivation, and oversaw a department of about 20 individuals. Mark was scheduled to be there at 1 PM. His resume looked great and he was ranked in the top ten candidates to interview.

Mark arrived ten minutes early- always a good thing. But what wasn't such a good thing, Mark brought his mother. Or more accurately, Mark's mother brought him. Kellie watched with curiosity as the mother parked the car and appeared to be giving him a pep talk. She then walked this thirty-something year old man to the office and announced his arrival. When Kellie came forward to introduce herself to Mark, the mother *licked her fingers and wiped down his hair* (just like you've seen in the movies!). As if that wasn't enough, the mother followed Kellie into the room for the interview.

The interview was short. Mark didn't get the job. And yes, his mother had prepared and submitted the resume for him.

Totally awesome employees have cut the umbilical cord. Their mom isn't attached at the belly and they have developed survival skills of their own. Totally awesome employees may love their mothers, may ask them for advice and counsel with them regularly. But they do not bring them to interviews. They do not appear to employers as small children incapable of facing the world on their own. When an employer sees a mother (or father, spouse, or best friend) in the background it screams *"I need to be babysat!"* No employer desires to be a babysitter.

Buford was the manager at a local camera shop. He came to work on his off day to grab some papers he had left. The store opened at 9 AM. He got there at 1 PM. The "Open" light was off. The printing machine had not been turned on. There were forty orders waiting to be fulfilled. The checklist was unchecked. And his employee was reading a book at the counter.

Buford ended up with one less employee that day.

Totally awesome employees don't need to be babysat. They know what's required of them and they do it regardless of who's there, or not there, to watch over them.

Employers expect the individuals they hire to act responsibly and with maturity, whether they are 16 or 70 or anywhere in-between. Totally awesome employees are self-managers. They take pride in being responsible for themselves and ensuring that their actions, even when unseen, are in line with and often exceeding the expectations laid out for them.

Totally Awesome Employees

Are Grateful

"I express gratitude at every opportunity and recognize the wonderful blessings in my life."

The unemployment rate in some areas of the United States is ridiculously high. Some argue that people purposely live off of unemployment and don't try to get jobs. It's true; some do. But *many* able-bodied and intelligent people are unsuccessfully looking for work, were laid off through no fault of their own and frequently shed tears of frustration.

Totally awesome employees are grateful every single day that they are employed. Even if it's not the most ideal or the most incredibly pleasant, they are grateful they have a job. Even if their paycheck isn't as high as they'd like or they don't get to utilize their full potential, they are grateful anyway. Even if their commute is far and they have a wall instead of a window in their office, they appreciate being employed.

I visited with a business manager during the course of writing this book. She told me one of the most annoying things she runs into is an employee who feels entitled. "They've done nothing but get hired and suddenly they're in my office making demands and complaints." Totally awesome employees recognize that employers are doing them a favor. Employers have lots of options and they choose to take a chance on the person they hire.

Totally awesome employees are grateful. That attitude of gratitude leads them to more success within the company and *more happiness* in their life.

Some jobs are temporary, seasonal employment or perhaps stepping stones to something greater. But totally awesome employees treat every job the same; they give 100% effort and loyalty to their employer. Whether it's delivering pizza in the evenings while they finish up college or working in a high rise building for a multimillion dollar company, totally awesome employees are grateful for the position and come each day ready to show that gratitude.

Totally Awesome Employees

Soar Above the Clouds

"I find great happiness in my employment. My happiness is contagious and spreads to all who are near."

We can't control our environment. We can't control the weather. We can't control our customers, bosses, vendors, suppliers, or co-workers. We don't have any say in the random accidents and inconveniences that may occur at any given time.

But we do have total control over one thing: *our attitude*. It's the only thing that is inherently and forever our own. Totally awesome employees fly high. They know that attitude determines altitude and they choose to soar above the clouds. By doing so, they aren't weighed down by the rain, hail, and gloomy skies below.

Jack started work with a new company. He had a gentle demeanor and wore a smile. On his third day of work a co-worker tossed a comment his direction that caught him off guard, "That smile will be gone soon. This place sucks the life out of people."

After a month of employment Jack's wife Susan noticed a change. Her once loving and upbeat husband was coming home cross. Anger and annoyance replaced the laughter and fun conversation that had always been present in their home.

During a calm moment, she gently asked Jack what was going on. He took a few minutes to reflect and realized that the co-worker's prophecy had come true. His smile was gone. He felt that life had been sucked right out of him.

Jack and Susan decided to counter-attack. Within only a week or two there was another dramatic change; this time for better. Jack was smiling again. He had energy and was soaring high. He was happy. His wife was happy. And so were a good share of others in his company.

What changed? His attitude did. He had determined to lift himself and others to greater heights.

The couple had come up with a simple plan. He was to use a positive affirmation any time he felt darkness start to creep in and his happiness level drop. His chosen statement was: "I find great happiness in my employment. My happiness is contagious and spreads to all who are near."

Along with frequent repetition of the positive affirmation, Jack and Susan set two other rules. One: He would make zero negative statements about the company or anyone associated with it (including co-workers, bosses, customers, etc); if he heard a negative statement he had to extend two positives in response. Two: He would make eye contact with and smile warmly at every person he associated with during the day.

The results were well beyond what either of them expected. His decision to lift himself out of the sucking whirlwind opened a portal through which others could escape as well. The dark and depressing environment gradually became one of light and enjoyment. Friendship and unity replaced backbiting and gossip. Smiles replaced scowls. Employee performance and satisfaction ratings both skyrocketed.

Jack eventually became the manager and had a team of employees who loved him.

Totally awesome employees soar to great heights. Although it's impossible to force others to fly, when enticed with the beauty of the skies they often follow. Totally awesome employees understand the power of attitude. It's either poison to self and others or it's pure and needed nutrition. It brings despair and darkness or it brings happiness and light. Totally awesome employees yield the power of attitude to bless themselves and those around them. When change is needed, the first thing that must change is attitude.

Melody Litton

Totally Awesome Employees

Tame Their Texting Tendencies

"I respect my employer and the policies that are in place. I stay focused on my job and the customers I serve."

Cell phones are great. They serve so many purposes and have made the world a much more convenient place to live. They make it easy to communicate and share information. They are wonderful and yet they are also the downfall of so many employees.

Julie manages a daycare center. She often walks in on preschoolers kicking and tackling one another while their "caregivers" are sitting in a corner with their cell phones in front of their faces.

As a customer, I've waited for long periods of time while employees focus on their phones. As a supervisor, I've witnessed neglect of important duties while individuals waste countless minutes and hours with phone in hand. As a co-worker, I've seen people hide in closets and bathrooms to get their electronic fix during work hours while trying to avoid being detected. And as a mother I've cried while holding a very sick child in an ER, waiting for a nurse to finish up a telephone conversation with her boyfriend.

Totally awesome employees know that when they are on the clock, their time belongs to their employer. Most employers have policies regarding cell phones, personal e-mail, and other electronic usage. There is good reason for those policies! A totally awesome employee respects their position, employer, customers, and co-workers enough to keep their cell phones put away.

Totally Awesome Employees

Never Cover Up Mistakes

"I embrace mistakes as an opportunity to learn and grow. I reflect maturity and integrity when mistakes are made."

Every employee is going to mess up at some point while on the clock. The difference between a typical employee and a totally awesome one is the way it's handled. Typical employees attempt to cover up their mistake. Totally awesome employees fess up and do what they can to make it right.

Trevor worked for a nursing home. One night while passing medications he administered the wrong pills to an elderly resident. In an attempt to avoid getting written up, not only did he not tell anyone, but he also documented that both residents had accurately received their medications. He took the pills that were supposed to be administered to the patient and flushed them down the toilet.

That night the first patient (who had received the incorrect pills) went into diabetic shock. The second patient (who had gotten no pills) had a cardiac arrest. If the error had been known, both patients could have received needed care before either of these events occurred.

Tracy was responsible for a big case. She had been gathering evidence for weeks and prepping a file to present to the court in defense of a client accused of murder. As an attorney in a big law firm she knew this could make or break her chance for promotion.

Melody Litton

In a rush, she left her file in the backseat of a cab. She never got it back.

Excuses and lies filled her mind. She desperately wanted to lay blame everywhere but upon herself. But Tracy was a totally awesome employee. She went to her employer and told the truth. Her employer, although upset and distraught over the lost file, didn't react in anger toward her. He instead thanked her for coming to him so quickly and then he immediately assigned a team of ten individuals to help her prepare for the court date. When her client came before the jury, he was acquitted. Tracy was granted a promotion within the firm.

Seth was a brick mason. His new employer had chosen to hire him after giving a call to his previous supervisor. When asked what Seth's best quality was, his supervisor had told the potential employer, "Seth is never late. He shows up every day and you can bet your right arm he's going to be early." Seth's first day on the job he pulled up at 5 AM to ensure he'd be plenty early for the 7 o'clock roll call. (Yes, he was a little extreme in his desire to be on time.) He decided to take a nap while waiting for the others to arrive. At 7:30 he rushed into work, late for the first time in his life. He told the boss the truth. Three others were fired that day for being late. Seth wasn't. His history, and his willingness to be honest, kept him from getting kicked out the door.

Totally awesome employees do not beat themselves up when mistakes are made. They don't freak out, hide the problem, or lie about how it occurred. They take responsibility for it and face whatever consequences come. By doing so, totally awesome employees reflect maturity and integrity; two qualities highly desired by employers.

Melody Litton

Totally Awesome Employees

Are Masters of Time

"I am aware of each minute and make it count. My time is invested, not spent."

George really despised his job. He came in ornery, made everyone around him miserable, and never stopped watching the clock. Minute after minute he saw the big hand move like molasses and wondered if the day would ever end.

Totally awesome employees watch the clock too. But their motive is very different than George's. They believe in making minutes count. When they're "on the clock", they are aware of how their time is being used.

Veronica was hands down the best employee Jason's company had ever had. She was never late, made great use of her time, and did it all with a smile. She was able to accomplish three times the work load of many of the other employees without sacrificing her sanity or any of her breaks. In fact, Veronica thoroughly enjoyed her breaks. She visited with co-workers, ate a yummy lunch, and during her 15 minute down time in the afternoon would often take a stroll in the warm sunshine.

Jason watched Veronica week after week. She excelled at everything she was assigned to do. His company was better because of her and he wanted more employees like her. He requested that she share her secrets during an upcoming weekly meeting.

Veronica shared only one secret. But it was a great one.

She introduced her co-workers to her philosophy of mastering time. She taught them to use time to their advantage and to the advantage of the company. She told them to *invest* their time rather than spend it. She shared her motto: "Be aware of each minute and make it count."

There are a lot of things that differentiate a good employee from a totally awesome one; but one of the biggest things is time management. We each have the same amount of time in any given day but totally awesome employees utilize that time like true professionals.

Diana, a supervisor of several employees, shared her thoughts on this topic, "Salaried employees are paid 40 hours regardless, but I would take an 8-hour super productive employee *any day* over one that puts in a ton of hours just to try to appear that they are dedicated. Don't be a martyr."

There are books you can read and classes you can take and lots of dollars you can spend learning time management skills and I vote you look into some of those options. But it all boils down to three things: planning; focus; practice.

Totally awesome employees think ahead; they plan what they're going to do with their time at work, what needs to be accomplished and how to best accomplish it. They plan out how to achieve what matters most to their employer. And they plan time to do the things that matter to themselves as well (calling home to check on the kids, visiting with a co-worker about a shared interest, checking out the new yummy-smelling restaurant with lunch specials down the street. . .).

Totally awesome employees are masters of time. They use time to their advantage by planning, prioritizing, and staying focused. Doing so leads them to greater productivity and less stress; it allows them to meet their own needs as well as the needs of their employer.

Employees are paid for their time; totally awesome employees show integrity by choosing to manage it well.

Melody Litton

Totally Awesome Employees

Can Pass a Drug Test

"My mind and body are clear and active. I am free of addictive and harmful substances."

There's a large retail store in a Midwestern state. They drug tested before hiring. They couldn't hire even a quarter of the people who applied. They solved the problem of not having enough employees by lowering their drug test standard. They got more employees. But those hired certainly didn't add anything to the quality of their company. In time, their store was known as the dump of the town and the only decent individuals who went there were those passing through who didn't know better.

Totally awesome employees can pass a drug test. They don't show up stoned, drunk, whacked-out, hung over, or stumbling. They respect themselves and their employer enough to ensure their mind and body is at its full potential.

Stacy worked at a small town gas station. One night she came in with a smile and a large water bottle. The manager waved goodbye and left. Stacy sucked her bottle and enjoyed her graveyard shift. Everyone who came in that night left with a smile. It turned out Stacy was in such a great mood she'd given away more than $600 in gas; no wonder customers left with a smile. When the manager showed up the next morning Stacy was asleep on the counter with her bottle empty. After a quick whiff he discovered that what she'd been drinking surely wasn't water.

Mack worked as a Paramedic. He was scheduled to be on the ambulance at 6 AM. At 11 PM the night before, his supervisor found him downing shots at the bar. It turned out Mack no longer needed to be on shift at 6 the next morning, or any other morning either. When heading to the bar he hadn't thought of the lives he was putting at risk by his actions.

Not always will intoxication or drugs lead to death or major financial disaster for self or company. But the risk isn't worth it. Totally awesome employees would never be under the influence of alcohol or drugs while on shift, no matter the type of employment. They pride themselves in having clear and active minds and offer their best at all times.

Totally Awesome Employees

Go Beyond the Call of Duty

"I rejoice in my ability to make an impact for good on those around me. I choose to go beyond what's expected."

All good employees do their job. They know what is expected and they do it. But totally awesome employees do more than what's expected. They take the initiative and go beyond the call of duty.

Jeff worked on a construction crew. He was quite unique in his line of work; he showed up every day and on time. He was always busy. When his boss came around the corner it would never fail; ten guys would be not even pretending to work but Jeff would be doing his job, and doing it well. One evening the boss had to leave early for a family emergency. He told everyone to go home despite a looming deadline, knowing that little got done when he wasn't around to put the smack down on his employees.

When Jeff's boss returned the next morning the construction site was clean. The job had been finished, two trailers worth of scaffolding and equipment had been loaded, and the cleanup was complete. The boss immediately knew who deserved his thanks and with tears he gratefully headed back to care for his family.

Willie is a firefighter. One night he was dispatched to the home of a ninety year old gentleman who had dropped a hot pad into his oven which then burst into flames. The fire was put out in exactly 20 seconds. But Willie stayed with the man for over four hours; his scheduled shift had ended minutes after the call had come in. Noting that the man was visibly shaken, Willie sat beside him and offered comfort. Even after the man was at peace, Willie stayed to listen to stories of his younger years and shared some laughs. He went beyond the call of duty.

Two nights later this man passed away. The daughter found the last line written in his personal journal: "Had a wonderful night. I started a fire and met a new friend."

Totally awesome employees go beyond the call of duty. They go the extra mile for employers, customers, co-workers and others. Employees can often get away with bare minimum, doing the least amount possible to get by. But bare minimum isn't memorable and it doesn't lead to awesomeness. Totally awesome employees run beyond the finish line placed by others and set new records.

Totally Awesome Employees

Listen and Learn

"With eagerness I listen and with confidence I learn.

I pursue life-long learning."

College is important. Technical training is wonderful. Specialized certificates and degrees look really great on a wall. But education isn't the same as experience and totally awesome employees recognize that.

Eddie worked at a power plant in Tennessee. He'd been a lead supervisor for 10 years, had worked at the plant for 25. New HR policy mandated that all employees holding supervisor status must have a minimum of a Bachelor's degree. Eddie was fired and a new graduate was hired. Two weeks later the power plant called Eddie, begging him to return and re-instating him to his supervisory position. Lucky for them, he didn't hold a grudge.

A degree or specialized certificate will often get you in the door, will convince a company to give you a chance or at least take a peek at your resume. Training and education is essential in today's world and it is a wonderful way to begin lifelong learning. However; totally awesome employees understand that education doesn't equal expertise. They are not under the guise that their official piece of paper means that they're all-knowing.

Totally awesome employees enter a new job with humility. Humility is not fear, weakness, apprehension, or self-doubt; rather, it is a willingness to be teachable. Totally awesome employees are confident and capable, but they're also eager to learn from those with more experience and knowledge. They understand that it will take time and effort to become truly proficient in their new position.

As employees choose to listen, observe, ask questions and practice their new skills, they become worthy of their title. Whether the title is Doctor, Dog Trainer, Lawyer, or Babysitter, an employee becomes worthy of it through time and practice, through humble learning and dedication to developing the needed skills and expertise.

When an employer, supervisor, or more experienced co-worker offers advice and instruction, the totally awesome employee listens with eagerness and appreciation. They ask questions and request clarification when something doesn't make sense. They continue lifelong learning. They are never simply content with the knowledge they have, but rather, always striving to build on their current foundation.

Totally Awesome Employees

Speak Up

"I value my thoughts, observations, and concerns. I present them in a way that ensures mutual respect."

Unless a problem is known, it can't be fixed. There's no use whining to co-workers about an issue and then pretending like everything is fine when the boss comes around.

Ricky worked in a factory with hundreds of employees. Every day throughout the building employees would gripe under their breath that they were cold. Groups of employees would huddle together in the break room and discuss what a crappy situation they were in, standing still hour after hour and shivering. Ricky would listen as they spouted off about how the owner didn't care about them, how the CFO was too cheap to pay the extra electric bill for heat, and how picked on they were. But when the supervisors came through or employee meetings were held, no one ever said a word about it.

Ricky was a quiet guy. He didn't participate in the complaining but his feet did get cold throughout the day. After a few weeks, he made a decision. He was going to talk to the boss about the temperature. He made an appointment to visit with his supervisor the next morning. The appointment lasted less than 5 minutes. Ricky: "Sir, the factory is quite cold. Several of us are getting chilled as we stand at our posts throughout the day. We would certainly appreciate it if something could be done to ensure the factory was a bit warmer." Supervisor: "That's not good. I had no idea. Thank you, Ricky, for letting me know." That was the end of the conversation. By the next day, the factory was warm.

Employers won't always respond so quickly and they may decide not to take action at all. But unless they know about a situation or concern there's zero percent chance that something will be done about it. No employer enjoys a complainer. However; presenting information to an employer with respect and civility is not the same as whining. Requesting something with respect is 100 times more likely to see results than whining, pouting, whispering, or feeling bad for yourself. Totally awesome employees speak up! And they do so with respect.

Totally awesome employees also speak up when they see potential benefit for the employer. Several years ago I read a newspaper article that I found to be completely fantastic. There was a man who worked for a large vehicle manufacturer. He noticed that a small part of the engine design wasn't really needed. It used a bit of extra metal and only a few minutes of labor but it served absolutely no purpose. He presented his thoughts to the lead supervisor. The supervisor chose to have the situation looked at. After a bit of analysis the engineers discovered the man was right, the part was unnecessary. This one observation and the man's willingness to present his thoughts to his supervisor saved the company millions of dollars a year. The man was praised and given a very pretty bonus.

When an employee speaks up about a difficult situation or concern, management often appreciates ideas to fix or improve the situation. An employee shouldn't simply drop it in the lap of management because they don't want to deal with it. Totally awesome employees collaborate ideas and brainstorm with management to come up with suitable solutions.

Whining is a waste of air. Potentially beneficial thoughts are useless if not spoken. Totally awesome employees use their air well and speak up when there is good reason to. Their thoughts are heard because they are presented intelligently and with respect.

Once a concern or idea is presented to an employer, a totally awesome employee respects the decisions of that employer. They know that sometimes even great ideas get thrown under the rug, and that's OK. What matters is that employees speak up when there is potential benefit or other valid reason. They do so with the intent of ensuring awareness of issues and making valid thoughts and ideas known.

Totally awesome employees value their thoughts, observations, and concerns. They present them in a way that ensures mutual respect.

Melody Litton

Totally Awesome Employees

Decrease Drama

"I am calm. I am peaceful. I am drama free."

Drama belongs on TV, not in the workplace. Totally awesome employees decrease workplace drama; they never add to it.

Susie loved attention. Day after day she couldn't say enough about her horrible life, bad boyfriend, and stupid car. She talked about her itchy skin, frizzy hair, and how her lipstick just wouldn't stay on for the whole 12 hours that it was supposed to. She gossiped about co-workers and employers. She'd flirt like a "hoochie momma" every time a male was near her and then whine about how everyone just wanted her for her body. She would stir every pot she could find, pitting one individual or department against another. Essentially, she drove everyone in her workplace insane with her drama and caused many unwanted headaches.

Jack worked in the same office but was Susie's opposite. People enjoyed having him in the office. He was respectful and although he often conversed with others, it was never to stir the pot or point fingers. He didn't go on and on about the injustices in his life or try to be the star in every conversation.

Jack was chill. Susie was more like a tight rope walker yelling from the sky "Look at me!" Totally awesome employees don't get high on drama. And they don't play a role in the drama others create either.

There are thousands, if not millions, of examples of employees hitting walls, punching people, breaking things, slashing tires, spitting in food, trashing offices, and throwing items at the wall; not to mention threatening, cursing, blaming, and shouting. A totally awesome employee will never be found doing any of these things. They aren't violent and they control their tempers.

Totally awesome employees know when to keep silent and recognize when to politely walk away. They intelligently deal with various situations and strive to contribute to creating an environment of respect. They know that the workplace isn't the place for drama.

Totally Awesome Employees

Radiate Respect

"I radiate respect through thought, word, and action. I esteem myself and others as individuals of great value."

This world is full of all kinds of people. Totally awesome employees show respect to each of them. When a totally awesome employee sees another human being, he sees someone worthy of respect. They recognize that in the workplace respect is of utmost importance. We're each in a different place in life; physically, financially, spiritually, emotionally, and mentally. No matter where someone falls in any of these categories, a totally awesome employee is going to treat them like gold.

Kevin was new on the sales floor of a large BMW dealership. One sunny afternoon a scruffy looking man came in with a dirty backpack and started walking around the cars. None of the other salesmen gave him more than a quick glance before going back to their conversation about the previous night's game. The owner told Kevin to ask the man to leave, concerned that he was a homeless person looking to cause trouble.

Kevin walked up to the man and offered a warm smile and friendly hello. He looked past the dirty appearance and locked eyes with the man and asked what he could do to help him. The man kicked the ground and mumbled that he would like to sit in the BMW on the show room floor.

Kevin felt compassion for this man. He excused himself for a moment and went to talk to his boss. He asked permission to spend a few minutes with the man and show him the vehicles. His boss snorted at him but extended permission on the grounds that Kevin was responsible for anything that came of it.

Two hours later this man bought three brand new high end BMWs with the cash he held in his dirty backpack. Kevin got a beautiful paycheck.

The scruffy man had purposely gone to the dealership looking as he did. He was a very wealthy businessman and wanted to see how he would be treated if he appeared as the opposite. His goal was to discover someone who deserved the commission from his purchase. The man had visited two dealerships prior to Kevin's and had nearly ended his quest.

Totally awesome employees radiate respect. The respect, compassion, and courtesy they extend to employers, co-workers, clients and others is never fake or in vain. The results are not always seen on a paycheck, but there are always positive consequences to showing respect. Totally awesome employees enjoy better relationships with those around them, more peace of conscious, happiness, and satisfaction with themselves and their employment.

Being respectful is always the right choice. Totally awesome employees would never think of telling bad jokes, using foul language, or making derogatory comments. They never degrade someone else or turn their noses up at others. They use their brains and mouths to uplift others rather than tear them down. They radiate respect at all times via both verbal and nonverbal communication. Perhaps swearing, off color jokes, derogatory comments, arrogance and self-important attitudes are commonplace in the world, but they do not belong in the workplace.

Totally awesome employees radiate respect and others respect them for it.

Totally Awesome Employees

Utilize Mind Power

"I keep my mind turned on and tuned in. I focus, plan, and achieve."

Totally awesome employees utilize mind power. They keep their brains turned on and tuned in.

I asked Angie, a motel manager, what she appreciates most about her employees. She referred to one in particular. "BranDee is totally, absolutely, completely, reliable. She also sees what needs to be done and does it." It would be hard to find better compliments.

BranDee utilizes mind power to foresee what her employer wants her to do. And she does it! Totally awesome employees always keep their eyes open and brains active. They don't twiddle their thumbs waiting to be told each time to take a step. They know what's expected and what's important, and they take action to get it done.

Our mind is powerful. We can use it to our advantage or disadvantage. We can use it to focus, plan, and achieve; or we can allow it to wander, go blank, and be useless. We can use it to keep our attitude high and our thoughts upbeat. Or we can use it to focus on the negative, causing both internal and external destruction.

An employer will often hire a less qualified applicant whom they feel might be a healthy and positive addition to the team because in the long run, they can teach just about anything but personality and attitude. A healthy and well utilized mind can make a large impact for good.

Totally awesome employees also utilize their mind power to work smarter, not necessarily harder.

Elena was a housekeeper. It took her three times as long to complete her assigned work as the other housekeepers and her employer wanted to know why. She told him she didn't know, that she kept busy the entire day and felt like she was working as quickly as she could.

Her employer started to observe her. Sure enough, Elena did keep busy. She was moving the entire day and rarely sat down. But she wasn't working smart. He watched as she went down the hall six times to retrieve needed items for one room. Rather than taking everything with her the first time, she was walking from one end of the hall to the other with one towel and then again with a set of sheets. That was followed by a trip to get the duster and then the vacuum and then the bathroom supplies. She would walk the hall one last time to get the mints for the pillows. What a waste of time and energy!

Employers appreciate employees who not only have brains, but utilize them well. Totally awesome employees keep their mind clear and focused. They proactively tackle each hurdle and accomplish each job without waiting to be begged, scolded or pushed. They think. They act. They're ahead of the game; always efficient. And they do it all with a smile!

Totally Awesome Employees

Respect Their Position

"I respect the position I hold and perform to the best of my ability."

I couldn't write the last chapter without including this one. Totally awesome employees do utilize mind power. They're proactive and think clearly. They take action and do their jobs well, often exceeding the expectation of employers. They see what needs to be done and get it done. But totally awesome employees respect their position, recognizing limitations and authority. Job descriptions, skill level, legalities, and level of authority stay in the forefront of a totally awesome employee's mind.

Susan worked in a busy office. She strived to work hard and be a great employee. While her boss was away on a business trip she noticed his files were not alphabetized and decided to work to get that fixed before he returned. She put off the checklist he'd left her, believing that this would take higher priority.

When he returned she showed him what she had done. He looked like the cartoons with steam blowing out of their ears. Before shooting through the roof, he gained his composure and spoke to her respectfully. She then spent the next seven days re-filing two thousand folders. They had been arranged according to date, not name. The names were of little consequence but the date was of utmost importance. In order to fix it, she had to go through the contents of each folder to find the date and then began the painstaking process of re-organizing them. And she wasn't paid for her time.

Employees don't know all of the reasons behind decisions that employers make. Sometimes policies and procedures don't seem to make sense and an employee may feel there's a better way. When such occasions arise, a totally awesome employee uses his mouth to find out why. He asks. When questioned with respect, most of the time an employer will give an answer. A good share of the time the response will make sense. Sometimes it won't. But once an employer has laid down a limitation or asked an employee to follow a particular policy, a totally awesome employee respects it.

Limitations are in place for the benefit of all. A nurse isn't allowed to prescribe medications, even if she knows what the patient needs. A doctor isn't allowed to give legal advice to a criminal patient, even if he has an educated opinion. A tax accountant can't act as a priest and marry a couple so he can put "married filing jointly" on their taxes to benefit them.

Employees may have many great ideas. But before acting on any idea, a totally awesome employee considers limitations and ensures that following through will be in the best interest of all involved. They respect each position they hold and by doing so, in time, they are able to achieve the titles and positions they desire.

Totally Awesome Employees

Have Short Noses

"I am a person of integrity."

I hope you've read the story of Pinocchio. It's a great one with many moral lessons to be learned. One of those moral lessons is that lying is bad. Pinocchio grows a long nose when he tells a lie. In time, lies become as apparent as though we were wearing them on our face. For awhile we may get away with a lie here and there, but it's never in our best interest. And it causes a lot more trouble than it solves. I have never met a person who enjoys being lied to. And I'm willing to bet that there isn't an employer who would knowingly keep a liar around for long.

Patrick really wanted to head out of the office and begin his holiday break. He had a stack of files still sitting on his desk he had agreed to complete and e-mail before leaving. He finished two out of two hundred and ninety files and decided that was good enough. He put on his coat and headed out the door. His supervisor hollered at him to have a great holiday and asked if the files were complete. He said "Absolutely! They're good to go. Have a happy Easter." And off he went. His supervisor checked with her other employees as they left and put in a final report to the lead supervisor that all was in order before she finally got to lock up and leave for the night.

After the holiday break is when his supervisor discovered the deceit. She was standing beside him and asked him to pull up the emails of completed files. She needed some information. When he opened his e-mail she saw two files, not the two hundred and ninety she expected.

Melody Litton

The company faced legal consequences due to his negligence and dishonesty. He was given a demotion and cut in pay. If I'd been his employer, he'd have been awarded a ticket out the front door.

Totally awesome employees don't lie. No matter the situation, totally awesome employees choose to be honest.

Along with telling lies, a big part of honesty is not being a thief. Employees often take home office supplies, add extra minutes to their time cards, eat food that is meant to be sold, give un-approved discounts to family or friends, use equipment, or find ways to gain more commissions than they've earned through sales etc. These employees don't often view themselves as thieves. According to the dictionary a thief is "somebody who steals something, especially one who intends to escape notice." So, if the dictionary is correct, any employee who takes more than they are granted by their employer, whether product, money, or time, is a thief. A totally awesome employee would never steal. An employee is entitled to only what is agreed upon between employer and employee; nothing more.

A person may be a good employee, a great one even! However, this doesn't mean they are entitled to anything more than their pay or what their employer gives them. Stealing not only gets someone fired, but it essentially makes them unemployable; and of course, totally *non-*awesome.

Now a word of clarification, being honest doesn't mean being tactless, brutal, or uncaring. It also doesn't mean being quiet about a paycheck that is incorrect or unfair. Totally awesome employees skillfully combine tact, kindness, intelligence, and honesty into a beautiful package. They speak up respectfully when compensation issues need to be addressed. They use honesty in all aspects of their job and in work relationships.

Totally awesome employees hold their head up high and display their nicely proportioned noses for the world to see. They aren't afraid of questioning or inspection because they have nothing to hide.

Melody Litton

Totally Awesome Employees

Model Modesty

"I dress, speak, and act in ways that reflect respect for myself and others."

Every day Yoli had to send employees home to change their clothing. She sent out dress policies regularly. Everyone signed them. Few followed them.

Brock had an interview for a job at a warehouse. He showed up wearing a dress shirt and slacks. Four other men were waiting for interviews in rough looking jeans and t-shirts. He wondered if he'd overdressed. But as he was leaving, the employer actually thanked him for dressing in a way that showed respect for the interview.

Totally awesome employees model modesty. Modesty is a term not used a lot in today's world. But it's important. Modesty is an attitude of propriety and decency in dress, language, grooming and behavior. It shows respect to self, employer, and others.

Breasts are awesome. I'm glad I have them. But breasts and cleavage don't typically belong hanging out of shirts in the workplace. Butts are great. People can even get implants now to pump them up a bit. But rear ends shouldn't be inching out of short skirts at the office and men's pants do actually belong above the cheeks.

Men look mighty fine in thousand dollar tailored suits. But a tailored suit may not be appropriate for a construction worker. Exotic dancers will have a different level of appropriate dress than bankers. Pizza delivery boys and servers at a high end restaurant will need to keep a slightly different wardrobe. Modesty in dress shows respect for yourself, employer, customers, and those you work with. Our clothing sends a message; the clothing of a totally awesome employee sends the right message.

Totally awesome employees don't stink. They shower and wear clean clothes. They do their hair and brush their teeth. They keep their nails clean and even check their ears for big chunks of wax. Modesty is more than covering up; it's caring for overall appearance and hygiene. The appearance of an employee is a reflection of the employer.

Olivia worked in a hardware store. She was the brunt end of constant jokes and harassment. She endured listening to endless vulgar language and words which made her shrink inside.

Modesty in language is even more overlooked than dress. Much is learned from the words we speak and language we use. Totally awesome employees avoid vulgar language and off-color jokes. They speak in a way that reflects intelligence and respect.

A totally awesome employee models modesty in hygiene, dress, language, and action. Their modesty makes them shine and sets them apart from a world often filled with filth and disrespect.

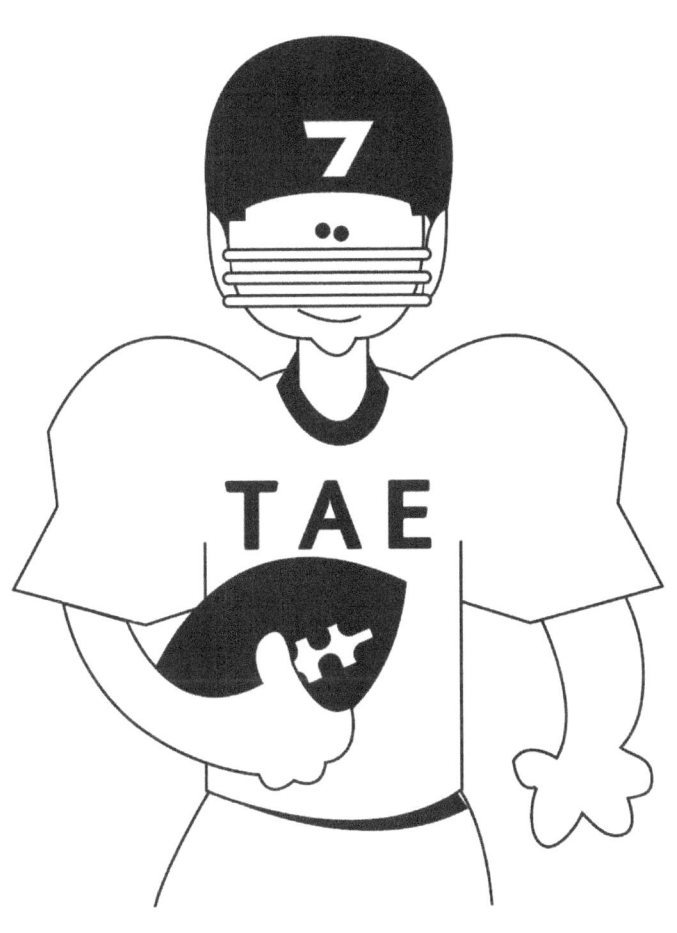

Totally Awesome Employees

Play for the Team

"I am a team player. I can be counted on to do my best and inspire others to do so as well."

Selfish people are definitely not totally awesome. People who concentrate only on their own needs, desires, best interest, and glory will never succeed at becoming totally awesome employees.

Brad loved to hog the spot light. Everything he did, he took credit for. Everything he didn't do, he took credit for. Anytime there was a success in the company, he deemed himself responsible. Anytime there was a failure, he was quick to aim his finger in another direction.

Brad fooled a manager here and there. He even got an extra pay raise and occasional promotion. But his self-focused attitude never fooled anyone for long. He didn't care about the company, his co-workers, or even the customers. He cared about himself.

Isabelle was dynamic and fun. She was the glue that held everyone else together. She could turn any group of individuals into a team; one that protected, helped, and looked out for one another.

Isabelle was known for the little things she did. When she was heading off shift, she was careful to prepare and lay out whatever might be needed by the next person coming on. They were always ahead because of her efforts and were grateful to her. She offered assistance and encouragement whenever she saw it might be needed. She spoke words of kindness to those who were down and words of love to those who were unkind. As a team leader she inspired individuals to do their best but never degraded them for weaknesses.

Totally awesome employees play for the team. They have the good of the company, their co-workers, and customers at the forefront of their mind. They accept and appreciate praise and acknowledgement, but never hesitate to spread that recognition to others as well. They inspire feelings of unity and support.

Totally Awesome Employees

Go with the Flow

"I skillfully adapt to every occasion. I face change and inconvenience with grace and confidence."

Totally awesome employees adapt to change. They are flexible when last minute changes or inconveniences occur. They don't flip out if their employer asks them to switch a shift. They don't go crazy if they have to do things slightly differently than has been done in the past. They don't have a heart attack when they get a new supervisor or are assigned to a new area.

Forrest has been with the same company 26 years. Managers have come and gone. Policies have changed and then changed back. Co-workers have left, died, been hired and fired. The walls in the office have been painted green, yellow, white, and striped. He's worked graveyards when scheduled for days and weekends when scheduled for weekdays. He's learned that "everything's gonna be alright." Forrest has gone with the flow for 26 years and he's figured out what all totally awesome employees know; nothing is worth flipping out about. Take things in stride, one day at a time. Ride the wave and enjoy it.

Knowing how to adapt and being willing to be flexible are incredibly helpful in the workplace. Employers appreciate an employee who goes with the flow. Not everything can be foreseen. Sometimes stuff comes up and plans change. Sometimes management decides to try something new. Sometimes disasters strike, fires start, tornadoes hit, coffee spills, and puppy dogs pee. We don't know exactly what we'll face each day, but totally awesome employees take it in stride. They adapt.

They bend, twist, swivel and turn in order to make things work.

Totally Awesome Employees

Make a Difference

"I make a difference for good."

Employees come and go. Some are great; others not so great. Some improve a company and others literally destroy it. Totally awesome employees always make a difference, a difference for good.

Brendon started with a grocery store pushing carts for $8 an hour. Now, he works as one of the store managers making $90,000 a year. Some of the others who were with him in the beginning are still making minimum wage.

Brendon is a totally awesome employee. When he was newly hired he made a decision; every day he came to work he was going to make a positive impact. He made customers smile and helped co-workers learn better ways of doing things. He respected management and wasn't afraid to discuss his ideas and suggestions with them. As he moved up the ladder from one position to the next his employee reviews contained comments such as "Brendon is a star employee. Our department has improved tenfold since he's joined our team." and "Brendon is a positive influence on all around him. He can turn even the grumpiest people into happy customers."

Totally awesome employees make a difference for good. They're noticed, even when they feel as though perhaps they are not. Even when others are stealing the limelight and taking credit when it's not due, in time the truth is shown. Employers know who is giving their all to the company and who is simply showing up for a paycheck.

Totally awesome employees shine, even when they don't mean to. It's really hard to hide total awesomeness and employers notice, appreciate, and reward it.

Choose to be a totally awesome employee. We each have the power to become whoever we want to be. It's my hope that we will strive to be awesome.

Totally awesome employees make a difference, a difference for good. As we soar above the clouds our perspective will become more clear.

Through our efforts, the workplace will become a better place to be. We will benefit and so will the world.

Awesomeness is always worth the effort. I wish you joy in your journey.

Power Statements

"I am the epitome of reliability."

"I radiate kindness and light to all around me."

"I am responsible and mature. I perform to the best of my ability at all times."

"I express gratitude at every opportunity and recognize the wonderful blessings in my life."

"I find great happiness in my employment. My happiness is contagious and spreads to all who are near."

"I respect my employer and the policies that are in place. I stay focused on my job and the customers I serve."

"I embrace mistakes as an opportunity to learn and grow. I reflect maturity and integrity when mistakes are made."

"I am aware of each minute and make it count. My time is invested, not spent."

"My mind and body are clear and active. I am free of addictive and harmful substances."

"I rejoice in my ability to make an impact for good on those around me. I choose to go beyond what's expected."

"With eagerness I listen and with confidence I learn. I pursue life-long learning."

"I value my thoughts, observations, and concerns. I present them in a way that ensures mutual respect."

"I am calm. I am peaceful. I am drama free."

"I radiate respect through thought, word, and action. I esteem myself and others as individuals of great value."

"I keep my mind turned on and tuned in. I focus, plan, and achieve."

"I respect the position I hold and perform to the best of my ability."

"I am a person of integrity."

"I dress, speak, and act in ways that reflect respect for myself and others."

"I am a team player. I can be counted on to do my best and inspire others to do so as well."

"I skillfully adapt to every occasion. I face change and inconvenience with grace and confidence."

"I make a difference for good."

Melody Litton is a happy and energetic woman. She recently celebrated eleven years of marriage to her favorite person in the world. She is the mother of four "totally insane yet awesome" children. She has a Bachelor of Science Degree from Southern Utah University where she studied Interpersonal Communication and Sociology. She is a Nationally Registered EMT. Melody also enjoys working with others in teaching stress relief techniques including energy medicine and visualization exercises.

Melody's goal in writing the *How to be Totally Awesome* series is to bring a little laughter and some positive changes into the world.

She sees our world as a great place and believes that with a little effort we can make it even better.